Married2TheMission:
BIRMINGHAM

A City Destined For Reform

by

SHADARIA A. ALLISON

Dedication

This book is dedicated to the beautiful souls that reside in Birmingham, Alabama. For Amun Lamare Blue.

For Angela Davis. For Kionna Glover. For Lanell Truss. For every person suffering from homelessness, drug addiction, and mental illness.

For Randall Woodfin. A brave young man who took on the desire to manage the city he loved in 2017.

For those who live under the false pretense that they have to work their way to God's love. For all of those who both dedicated and lost their lives in the beautiful struggle that was the "Civil Rights Movement."

For Loveman's Village, Gate City, Southtown, and all other urban housing developments in Birmingham, AL.

For the future hope of Carraway Hospital.

ForMarried2TheMission. For JESUS, The Love of my life.

Birmingham, this one's for you.

"One cannot succeed at reformation...without recreation."

-Shadaria A. Allison

CHAPTERS ON CHANGE

Changing History:

"The History of Birmingham."

Changing The Church:

What did Jesus really say?

Changing Educational Structures in Birmingham:

"Improving the learning class of ALL students"

Changing Transportation:

"A vision that will change the way we move"

Changing What We Say:

"Words of Affirmation in Birmingham"

Changing Community Involvement:

"Sincere reform through the power of recreation"

Married2TheMission:

"Women's Recreation and Recovery"

"You're blessed when you're at the end of your rope. With less of you there is more of God and his rule.

"You're blessed when you feel you've lost what is most dear to you. Only then can you be embraced by the One most dear to you.

"You're blessed when you're content with just who you are—no more, no less. That's the moment you find yourselves proud owners of everything that can't be bought.

"You're blessed when you've worked up a good appetite for God. He's food and drink in the best meal you'll ever eat.

"You're blessed when you care. At the moment of being 'care-full,' you find yourselves cared for.

"You're blessed when you get your inside world—your mind and heart—put right. Then you can see God in the outside world.

"You're blessed when you can show people how to cooperate instead of compete or fight. That's when you discover who you really are, and your place in God's family.

You're blessed when your commitment to God provokes persecution. The persecution drives you even deeper into God's kingdom. -Jesus

Gospel of Matthew 5:3-10 (The Message Version)

#LOVE

Love.

They say that love is an intense affection for someone or something. It covers all wrongs, suffers long, and is centrally motivated by a variant of emotions and commitment.

Sometimes, love can lead us into places that we would have never expected to be in order to bring both change and influence to things or more importantly, people.

This is my complete and utter sentiment of Birmingham, Alabama.

I am not sure when I fell in love with Birmingham. It was something that just happened. I moved here as a teenager from Brooklyn, NY. with hopes of leaving as soon as I finished high school to indulge in an adventurous life of *vain* stardom.

Instead, I became the product of a place with strong historical influence, rich in southern custom, and in **desperate need of reform.**

With every old building in an improper place, every run-down recreational facility, and in the bright eyes of every child growing up in the projects in Birmingham, I saw how desperately I wanted to be apart of the culture that would bring life to the "canvas" Birmingham truly is.

I became steady with the city. Engaged to its purpose. Married2Themission.

1

Changing History: *"The History of Birmingham."*

To establish reform in any city, you must address the aching reality of what has prevented its overall success.

Questions have to be asked and answers have to be visible.

What is draining the "life" out of a place? What has happened there? What seems to be the "constant theme" throughout its lifespan?

Asking these questions can begin a movement of revitalization that has never been seen before.

"Sometimes the way out to the future is by glancing over the shoulders of the past." - Shadaria Allison

THE INVISIBLE HAND

Stronghold's or "authorities" are often established in 5's.

Similar to a human fist, five fingers are needed to grasp hold of any object.

The same can be demonstrated throughout the territory of any metropolis.

In Birmingham, the strongholds that stagnate growth are obvious: **Racism, Poverty, Division, Religion, and Murder.**

Racism:

Prejudice, discrimination, or antagonism directed against someone of a different race based on the belief that one's own race is superior. *(Google Public data, 2017)*

Birmingham, Alabama was founded by Englishmen in 1871. Hoping to mock the success of the city from whence its name was inherited; Birmingham, UK; Birmingham was meant to be an epicenter for the steel and mining industry.

Largely built upon this intent; Birmingham became just that.

An industrial competitor of its day, the city was known for manufacturing cars and railroads, coining itself "the magic city".

However, just like any other city in the rural South; Birmingham was built on the backs of underprivileged African American farmers, employees, and child labor; all at the lowest rate possible.

For years to come, Birmingham remained at the center of racial tension. At the center of fights for equal education, voting rights, and ultimately the fight to survive. At its core, Birmingham became the *'center capital'* for murder, segregation, and racial disturbance.

Tensions often failed to disbond as African Americans were determined to fight for social and civil freedoms; erupting finally into one of the most meaningful movements in American history, the "Civil Rights" Movement.

Aside from death, social devastation, and subtle hints of reform in various locations throughout Birmingham; The Civil Rights Movement proved that even in "shattering the glass" of racial hatred in Birmingham, *the **debris** never left the city.*

Debris in Birmingham = Poverty.

Poverty: The state of being inferior in quality or insufficient in amount. *(Google Public data, 2017)*

From the dawn of its existence, Birmingham has prided itself on being a city built by **wealthy means and poor people**.

Structured education, lack of both medical and educational resources, coupled with impoverished housing developments built more like a ***unique concentration camps***; all seem to be the premier culture in BIrmingham.

Boarded by ,*"citizen ancestors"* from the *"white flight"*, Birmingham desperately suffers from the inability to benefit from equal distributions of information, housing, counsel, or funding.

Mountain Brook, Hoover, Vestavia, and other neighboring communities throughout Birmingham, look almost unrecognizable in comparison to its alternative ***"sister communities"*** such as: West-End, Ensley, and North Birmingham.

This is undeniably intentional in order to keep the wealth in the hands of those who inherit it, and to completely shut out the resource of provision and education to minority communities in Birmingham.

Wherever you find racism and poverty there will be an undeniable amount of ***division.***

Division: The action of separating something into parts, or the process of being separated. A disagreement between two or more groups, typically producing tension or hostility.
(Google Public data, 2017)

"Wherever there is bitterness, envy, and strife there will be every evil work present".- James 3:16 (paraphrased)

In its attempt for social reform and complete freedom, Birmingham has become the "poster child" for division.

Primarily, because one sector of people believe that the "old way" of establishing and meeting needs is better than the ability to have basic human resource and rights for all.

When hate and poverty are infused into various communities within the confines of a metropolis such as Birmingham; the people begin to believe what they have been shown.

Some of us, and only some of us matter in Birmingham.
Some of us, and only some of us deserve proper education.
Some of us, and only some of us are worthy of a good life.
Some of us, and only some of us are worthy of love.
Some of us, and only some of us are better than the others because of the color of our skin.

One can only imagine the hurt, the pain, and the bitterness that comes with being alive post civil destruction in such a small city.

The results of division in Birmingham have caused a sense of self-hatred that has manifested itself in uncanny variances: **homelessness, gossip, drug addiction, and violence.**

One community hates the other.

East side "beefs" with the West. Out-skirted cities that nest Hoover residents get premier education, while the inner city students suffer. One section of town is better than the next but on Sunday, we can all sit together.

After all, there ain't nothing like good-ole' southern religion.

Religion: The belief in and worship of a superhuman controlling power, especially a personal God or gods.
(Google Public data, 2017)

Whether it was a hub for political planning to escape the chains of oppression during the "Civil Rights Movement."

OR

A masonic temple to secretly assemble. All while worshiping "God knows what" for "God knows what".

OR

Private Wiccan assemblies.

OR

Neighborhood Mosques and other creative temples.

OR

A pentecostal southern Baptist, Anglican, Methodist, Catholic, AME Zion, Church of God, COGIC church; (all denominations and religious sectors not listed.)

Religion has always been a dominant culture in Birmingham.

At the exasperation of counting, I am sure that there are several hundreds of local churches throughout Birmingham.

Religion to Birmingham is as complementary as ketchup is to a hotdog.

Why is this a problem?

Resting on the backs of division, Religion without a true spiritual connection to God, breeds more division. - Shadaria

No one can associate an all loving God with hatred, lynching, murder, racism, and injustice.

A city that claims to unify under God socially, without deliberate "fruit" of that belief is essentially lacking a moral compass. Let alone, a REAL relationship with him.

Anywhere lacking a real relationship with God, is birthing hatred by the minute.

Anywhere birthing hatred by the minute, is birthing **murder** by the second.

Murder:

The unlawful premeditated killing of one human being by another. (*Google Public Data 2017*)

Birmingham History: Unjust violence and murder.
Birmingham Present: Unjust violence and murder.

I guess when you train a culture up in murder teaching them that hatred is the anecdote for its existence, it perpetuates that same mentality generationally.

People were killed unjustly then. They are killed unjustly now.

As of 2017, Birmingham AL has topped lists in America for some of the highest murder rates in the nation.
Featured on the "first-48", a murder series aired on A&E, Birmingham has become more famous for murder than it has for owning national monuments in its downtown sector.
The youth are hurting.
The teens are on drugs.
Gun access is easy.
Policing is hard.
Self Hatred is real.
Racial Hatred is severe.
Birmingham is experiencing an "cultural eclipse", when it should be *singing the praises of great reform.*

"My people perish from a lack of knowledge."

Hosea 4:6 (paraphrased)

2.

<u>Changing The Church:</u> *What did Jesus really say?*

The Jews then responded to him, "What sign can you show us to prove your authority to do all this?" Jesus answered them, "Destroy this temple, and I will raise it again in three days."They replied, "It has taken forty-six years to build this temple, and you are going to raise it in three days?" But the temple he had spoken of was his body. **- John 2: 18-21 NIV**

As Christians, we all say and believe with sharp emotional conviction,that we want to be like Jesus.
Never truly understanding what that means, we fall desperately short in our role as **"the church".**

All at once, our christian faith has become but an allegory-like competitor for other religions to mock. Could it be that the reasoning lies in our ability to avoid the needy? Lacking compassion beyond palladium sized pulpits, and shunning the "least-of-these" grafted in the culture of Birmingham?

Can I preach?

BRACE YOURSELF! This perspective will go beyond your local service days.

It will venture past your neighborhood once-a-month "community cookouts."

It will nest beyond the *typical* social media rants, and sold out conferences.

This is KINGDOM!

As mentioned before, Birmingham is the "mecca" for organized religion.

 Churches have to make up at least 55% of real estate in the city (educated guess) and yet,*I've never seen so much miss-fortune, so much pain, so much debt, so much division, so much gossip, so much homelessness, so much drug use, so much hopelessness, so many troubled youth to saturate throughout a city, the way I have seen in Birmingham, AL.*

All this power? All the laying on of hands? All the tongues, and shouting,and no one can produce reform?

Despite the <u>MILLIONS</u> of dollars that pour into a house we call "church", no HOMELESS FACILITY is located in any of them?

There are some churches here that hold real estate in over eight communities in Birmingham, yet not one hosts an...

ON CAMPUS HOMELESS SHELTER!!
A DRUG REHABILITATION CENTER!
A PLACE FOR RUNAWAY TEENS?
A HOUSING DEVELOPMENT PLAN FOR DISPLACED MILLENNIALS?

NO PLACE FOR THE MENTALLY ILL?, BUT WE HAVE CHURCHES EVERYWHERE!??????!!!!!!!!!!!!!!!!!

THE CHURCHES THROUGHOUT BIRMINGHAM ARE HOLDING A GOLDMINE IN WEALTH !! YET WE ARE THE LAZIEST HUMANITARIANS THERE ARE IN OUR OWN COMMUNITIES!
YOU TELL ME WHERE GOD IS PLEASED WITH THAT?
FURTHERMORE, CAN YOU TELL ME WHERE THIS LOOKS ANYTHING LIKE JESUS?!!!!!!!!

 The majestic King that rules over the world knew that the only way to redeem earth would be to experience it himself. He put down his gold and splendor to make himself known amongst a people that he created, yet knew would reject him.

Present day, church has armor bearers, select seating assemblies, and once-in-awhile, church carnivals in hopes to SAVE BIRMINGHAM?

HOW COMICAL!!!

Who will go out, to BRING in?

Ever caught a fish inside of a building? Me either.

Who will sacrifice the plush living of preaching to be a true disciple? Who will be what JESUS has really called the church?

THE KINGDOM OF GOD CHARGED TO SUFFER VIOLENCE IN ORDER TO TAKE IT BY FORCE?!!!!!!

JESUS' MANDATE

The Spirit of the Sovereign Lord is on me,

because the Lord has anointed me

to proclaim good news to the poor.

He has sent me to bind up the brokenhearted,

to proclaim freedom for the captives

and release from darkness for the prisoners,

to proclaim the year of the Lord's favor

and the day of vengeance of our God,

to comfort all who mourn,

and provide for those who grieve in Zion—

to bestow on them a crown of beauty

instead of ashes,

the oil of joy

instead of mourning,

and a garment of praise

instead of a spirit of despair.

They will be called oaks of righteousness,

a planting of the Lord

for the display of his splendor.

They will rebuild the ancient ruins

and restore the places long devastated;

they will renew the ruined cities

that have been devastated for generations.

ISAIAH 61:1-4

KINGDOM COME

Jesus had a plan for complete and total reconciliation, and restoration. *There was nothing in his plan that looked like distant love and popular trends.* The primary agenda for the establishment of his house was an all out REGIME.

The movie "Taken" starring Liam Neeson features the plot of a father that has to over the phone, witness the startling kidnapping of his daughter by sex trafficking hoodlums. I am convinced we need the same passion as the body of christ.

The event turns him into a beast. The pain from hearing his daughter bound, taken against her will, and then ultimately kidnapped turns one man into an army.

He leaves his home, and goes across the world to a foreign country in order to find her.

He searches, asks, he terrorizes; even kills! All in the fearless effort to retrieve his daughter back from the hands of the enemy.

PICTURE THIS KIND OF REDEMPTION WHEN YOU THINK ABOUT THE SPIRITUAL COALITION THAT IS NEEDED IN THE STREETS OF BIRMINGHAM, ALABAMA!

Nowhere in our "biblical arsenals" did Jesus ask for a clean cut version of his love for us. His parables always beckon the lost into fellowship with him that suggests an incomparable closeness like one has never seen.

Jesus made it ultimately clear that his mission was to save, and then ton empower his children in begetting more children to inherit the ***"kingdom"*** of God. He wanted us all to be reconciled to him in a facet that seemed radical, loving, and intentional.

He is calling us as believers in Birmingham to the same mission.

STOP ATTENDING THE PHYSICAL CHURCH WITHOUT IN-COMPASSING THE "CALL" OF BEING THE <u>LITERAL CHURCH.</u>

Stop telling troubled youth and adults that all they need to do is "go to church", and "pay their tithes". Stop being a false witness by speaking so eloquently about a God *in heaven* that you fail to love people through on earth.

The bottom line is this:

WHEN SOCIAL CLIMATES NEED SHIFTING, NO MATTER WHO STANDS IN THE POLITICAL OFFICE, THE MEMBERS OF THE LORD'S KINGDOM ARE TO BE AT THE FOREFRONT.

 Even if the forefront is behind the scenes.

"Then if my people who are called by my name will humble themselves and pray and seek my face and turn from their wicked ways, I will hear from heaven and will forgive their sins and restore their land." 2 Chronicles 7:14 NLT

The assumption is not that all we have to do is pray, but rather that we add prayer with a deliberate effort to restore the ruins established by the enemy in our city.

Politely stated: It's time to get off of our butts, and get busy.

It's time to become integral with our earnings!
It's time to nurture the broken!
Feed the hungry!

Bandage the WOUNDED!

Counsel the weary!

Resource and educate the needy!

Enlarge kingdom territory!

Be present in government!

Be a REAL hand in the community!

The primary reason the world succeeds more at humanitarianism
than we do is because they SHOW UP MORE THAN WE DO!

**STRIP YOUR MAN MADE TEMPLES DOWN, AND
TURN MY FATHER'S HOUSE BACK INTO A PLACE FOR
HIS CHILDREN, OR RETIRE!!!!!!!!!!!!!!!!!!**

P.S.

"Yeah...I said it."

3.

Changing Educational Structures in Birmingham:

"Improving the learning class of ALL students"

Imagine having two children. One lives in the suburbs, the other in the city. The child in the suburbs enjoys everyday living, clean communities, accessible recreation, and countrysides.

Meanwhile, the child living in the city enjoys the skylines, festivals, and urban culture.

Tell me, who deserves the better education?

The short answer is, ***both of them.***

Somewhere along the lines, Birmingham has desperately missed this realization.

The painful perception in the city of Birmingham, is that if you don't live on the "better" outskirts of the city you dont deserve better education. This has been an aching reality for years.

Could it be that the venom of segregation is more potent because it is implemented throughout early childhood education and development?

Being on both sides of the coin, I've observed that suburban communities have been offered twice as much as Birmingham City School students in the realms of advancing education.

Structuring:

I remember being a teenager growing up in the Hoover City School system.
Hoover, known for its safe neighborhoods, great education, and reliable community police, has remained a reputed staple throughout Alabama for years. True to its fragmented state, Hoover is its own municipality, even though it nests less than 15 minutes outside of downtown Birmingham.

Growing up in Hoover, the resources were endless. The buildings were beautiful. The ***bias was obvious***.

I quickly made friends with inner city Birmingham students, and when I would mention where I attended school; it was always the same reaction: "You all think you're better"! "Excuse- me", or "Are you rich?"
It saddened me to see that in order to receive a better education in Birmingham, you had to live outside of the city.

Why were we given laptops, and they given broken textbooks?
Why did we have state of the art institutions, and they given barely running facilities?
Why were we given top security, and they "crime raided" schools?

I guess being the right color, and having the right amount of money can buy a higher learning?

What is the resolve?

Recreation. Community Involvement, and Resources.

As we all know, children have been shaping our world for centuries. Every leader, president, and entertainer have all been shaped by their childhood. Keeping that in mind, every child no matter color, belief, sex, or neighborhood deserves the best ethic there is to offer in education.

To place a lack of value in any child's education is an insult to humanity, and more importantly to GOD!

Matthew 19:14 King James Version (KJV)

... But Jesus said, Suffer little children, and forbid them not, to come unto me: for of such is the kingdom of heaven.

Do we really believe that a loving God would make resources unattainable to a certain child based on where they live? Or the color of their skin?

Absolutely not!

Birmingham, having the culture, buildings, and resources could be a place that flourishes with top of the line learning facilities that can teach our children in safe environments.

Not only in our city, but in the world.

Yet, without the community's help in development; I'm afraid our schools are in danger of becoming 'charity swaps' instead of places where we are can educate and develop future entrepreneurs, chemists, or even Presidents.

As mentioned before, a lot of Birmingham City School students live in communities that stand in complete contrast of the neighborhoods on the outskirts of Birmingham.

There have been many tests ran that show that even plants thrive in environments where there is safety, cleanliness, and beauty.

Why not our children? Are they not more valuable than plants?

Each school system needs to mirror the availability of premier standards that larger cities have: a reputable "creative arts" program, technology and engineering, foreign language, business ethics, forensic science, criminal justice, and medicinal healing.

If we are honest, Birmingham education seems to be stuck in a time warp, and is doing nothing for the love of our children who dare to dream.

If money is to be spent anywhere in this city outside of the growing business culture, education has to be a top priority,if we ever expect to see children excel, families decline in relocation, and our future more stabilized, we have to change the educational structures, now.

4.

Changing Transportation:
"A vision that will change the way we move"

In 2005, I took my first professional job at a world renowned hospital; UAB Medical Hospital, downtown Birmingham. As a teen-mother working there seemed to be an accomplishment professionally, but a chore as it pertained to transportation. I didn't have a car, so I had to rely upon the unreliable transportation system in Birmingham.

Sure, at face value it may seem like a small deal, but if I didn't leave an hour early every day and plan to stay an hour late,I wasn't a friend of luck in the "Magic City."

The headache of the struggle to get to work on time vexed me. I often found myself saying: "If only Birmingham were Brooklyn, I'd be to work early."

BIRMINGHAM THE NEW BROOKLYN?

My younger years in Brooklyn were fun. I don't know whether it was the people, clothes, or the culture, I just loved Brooklyn.

The whole world seemed at my fingertips. All it took was permission, a 'Metrocard', and a train.

Birmingham, famous for its mining, steel, and railways could stand to make in the "UPPER MILLIONS", if it would put the old rails to some use with a world class transit system.

With one willing decision to improve local transit, Birmingham would literally revitalize every school, town, and business surrounding the city.

How?

Transit will provide ...MONEY!

Running a dependable transit system would put this city back to work so fast, our heads would spin.

There are so many people that cannot afford, or do not have the financial means to maintain the responsibility of owning a car. In turn, paying a train fare for reliable transportation would be a great alternative for low income families.

Especially those who have to travel 10-25 miles outside of their residences to their jobs.

Imagining that Birmingham nests over 50 percent of individuals that do not own a vehicle, at a rate of two to four dollars per fare, Birmingham, could look to produce millions of dollars into the city in no time.

The transit system would also serve as a silent mediator for fragmented outskirts of the city, by bridging a direct monetary benefit per traveler.

Tourists would buy into it because of its eccentricity and innovation.

Transit would bring in ...JOBS

The solution of reliable transit would be a lucrative one, if Birmingham is looking to put its residents back to work.

From the mapping of its hub stations and locations, to the staffing of its subways, security, driver's, engineering, and maintenance, building a transit system in a place like Birmingham would put the entire city to work, and attract tourism for years to come.

The project would "shut the mouths" of those who suggest that the only way to materialize wealth in a city is a lottery.

Transit would bring in ...Health and Recreation.

Imagine a transit system that aided in health by creating a reason to walk longer distances.

The excitement of building new recreational facilities throughout Birmingham would put a spin on both the need and want for transportation as the exciting new transit system would awaken leaders and non profit organizers to show the youth new ways to travel.

Simply put, a transit system in Birmingham, would change how people looked at the south, **FOREVER**!

I see the money. Can You?

5.
Changing What We Say:
"Words of Affirmation in Birmingham"

BIRMINGHAM IS SET FREE FROM BONDAGE

BIRMINGHAM IS DRUG FREE

BIRMINGHAM IS PRODUCTIVE

BIRMINGHAM IS PLENTIFUL

GOD LOVES BIRMINGHAM

BIRMINGHAM IS THRIVING

BIRMINGHAM IS A GREAT PLACE TO LIVE

BIRMINGHAM IS A HISTORY CHANGER

BIRMINGHAM IS BEAUTIFUL

BIRMINGHAM IS INNOVATIVE

BIRMINGHAM IS BRILLIANT

BIRMINGHAM IS LOVE

BIRMINGHAM IS HEALED

**BIRMINGHAM WILL BE ONE OF THE GREATEST CITIES
TO LIVE IN**

BIRMINGHAM IS FREE FROM MURDER

BIRMINGHAM LOVES ITS PEOPLE

BIRMINGHAM LOVES ITS POOR

BIRMINGHAM LOVES ITS LEADERS

BIRMINGHAM LOVES THE COMMUNITY

**BIRMINGHAM LOVES AND GIVES WORLD CLASS
EDUCATION**

**BIRMINGHAM WILL BE KNOWN FOR LOVE AND NOT
HATE.**

6

Changing Community Involvement:
"Sincere reform through the power of recreation"

Recreation: the action or process of creating something again.

As a makeup artist, one of the most important yet fulfilling aspects of my job is bringing out the beauty in people who never imagined themselves as beautiful.

I share the same sentiment as it relates to the city of Birmingham.

Community Involvement

I believe it to be a total shame that helping has become such a scarce cliche' that people regard community service as a "glorified hobby", instead of a necessity.

While serving communities here in Birmingham, I have found that we have become so *"business oriented"* that we forget that some of the most important people in our city are the the ones who can't even afford to have an opinion. In other words, **the poor, the mentally ill, and the drug addict**.

The Poor

Driving through the streets of Birmingham, you may find yourself having the *erie feeling* that you are unintentionally apart of history.

Bronze statues of Martin Luther King, signs that landmark the footprints of Civil Rights leaders, and a celebrated display of Birmingham natives, such as: Eddie Kendricks; give you feeling of distinction.

Yet even the beauty of historical victories in our metropolis seem to fade in comparison to the sight of the poor people in Birmingham.

Its heartbreaking.

The only thing to compare it to is the likeness of a woman walking "shamefully nude" in winter, while everyone looks on refusing to cover her.

I am willing to bet that there are more poor people among us than we care to realize. There are so many poor people that the poorest are flamboyantly walking the streets everyday sheltering themselves in abandoned buildings daydreaming it would change into a place where they could just grab a nap.

I can remember serving at one of the prominent men shelters downtown Birmingham.

A few friends and I decided to eat lunch with some of them, while passing along the message of "hope" as we did often.

One of the young men there walked up to me and began to tell his story.
He ended up homeless after serving a long sentence in prison for avenging his sister who was brutally raped.

"I ain't no bad man", he explained.
Quietly listening, I felt the pain in his heart. I began to ask myself, why should one of many men go unresourced, minimally sheltered, and barely fed because of one mishap he made long ago in a regretful attempt to bring justice to his sister?

"I ain't no saint", I responded.
We took hands and prayed. We talked about God's love.

"Are you a pastor"?, he asked.
"No". I responded.
"I just care".

Shouldn't we all?

The Mentally Ill

In 2016 I decided to study Mental Health. Having a long battle with ADHD, I was curious to learn what exactly took place in the mind of the mentally ill.

Upon my research and later certification in Mental Health Studies; I found that some of the same triggers of poverty and homelessness share in similarities with the mentally ill.

Poor nutrition, trauma, genetics, and the lack of accessibility to proper resources, and/or health care.

Similar to the homeless in our city, mentally ill residents are numerous.

They can be found on the corners wandering, in parks, even in the hospital lobbies trying to access the best way to get free from the prisons in their minds.

If only they could afford to.

Ironically, there are some who take their health deficit and use it to express themselves creatively.

Lynn Park, a popular monument park downtown Birmingham hosts a great deal of both homeless and mentally ill residents.

While going there to serve I often found myself in conversation with some of the most talented homeless, and mentally ill people Birmingham has ever seen.

They would sing, laugh, write, draw and create art work. Often sharing ideas back and forth with one another until sunset came and each scattered to their own places of shelter.

To myself I would say if we only had places and programs strong enough in place to shelter, nurture, and cultivate their talents; these people could change not only Birmingham, but the world.

The Drug Addict

Drug use is becoming a social epidemic in America as a whole. However, when it hits close to home; the reality of the need for rehabilitation where you reside becomes sobering.

 Serving the community opens your eyes to the issues cities try to hide in marketing. We put pictures of cityscapes, new restaurants, and new real estate without showing the reality of the citizens.

THERE ARE MORE YOUTH AND PEOPLE ON DRUGS THAN WE CAN EVER REALLY KNOW IN BIRMINGHAM.

The shelters and hospitals have become so filled with drug users in our metropolis that we could stand to have a hospital and shelter just for them.

I believe the causes that fuel drug use are the same things that aid in homelessness, and mental illness.

LACK OF RESOURCES, TRAUMA, ENVIRONMENTAL UNDERDEVELOPMENT, LACK OF STATE-OF-THE ART RECREATIONAL FACILITIES, EDUCATION, AND SINCERE PARTICIPATION FROM "THE CHURCH".

Drugs are becoming more available, more accessible, and OVERLY AVAILABLE TO OUR YOUTH!
If we don't help out now, Birmingham communities will continue to suffer.

WE NEED MORE FACILITIES.
WE NEED BETTER HEALTHCARE.
WE NEED REAL HELP.
WE NEED MORE MONEY.
WE NEED BETTER EDUCATION.
WE NEED CHANGE.
WE NEED IT NOW!

WHAT IS MARRIED2THEMISSION?

MISSION STATEMENT

Married2TheMission is a non-profit organization whose sole purpose is to promote and celebrate the welfare and success of all women by the way of community service, outreach, and counsel.

To re-establish identity and purpose to those who find themselves lost. To be DELIBERATE resource to the broken, and less fortunate woman. To aid in spiritual, mental, and emotional breakthrough and support.

To provide shelter, rehabilitation, and recreation to those in need; that all may regroup, and be placed into society as functioning and stabilized citizens.

TO SERVE. TO UPLIFT. TO ENCOURAGE. TO CHANGE THE WORLD; ONE WOMAN AT A TIME.

You are WORTH IT!!

7.

Married2TheMission:

"Women's Recreation and Recovery"

2012 was a very hard year for me.

I had experienced some of the worst that life had to offer , and was ready for change.

Homelessness, teen pregnancy, and bad relationships would be the culprit in helping me to realize that not only did I need more but, that I deserved more, and more importantly that there were too many women who shared in stories just like mine.

This realization impregnated me with vision.

While riding two minutes north of downtown to my son's daycare in Norwood; a community in Birmingham, I happened to glance at this huge abandoned building by the name of Carraway Hospital.

The building seemed to have sturdy foundations, and stretched for what seemed like miles across illuminating grass.

Amongst the shattered glass and graffiti spray painted exteriors, I fell in love with Carraway Hospital.
"One day", I said to myself I will do BIG things here.

Married2TheMission

The years went on, and I still found myself dreaming of a way to help women.

In the middle of writing my first book **"Wise As A Serpent Harmless As a Dove: A woman's Manual"** I realized that I had a specific call to the welfare of women. I didn't know how to frame what I wanted to do. All I knew was that I didn't want to see another teen girl pregnant.

I didn't want to see another woman abused or homeless.

 I didn't want to see another me.

While on the phone with a friend I mentioned to her that I was done trying to make bad relationships work.

I was done playing less than, and that my place in this world was to do the mission that God created me for.

"I ain't worrying bout no man"!, I said.

"If anything, I'm Married to, it's the mission"!

"Nita"!, I yelled; That's it!

"Married2TheMission"!

I said we are gonna help women, and call it "Married2TheMission."
From then on, that is what we called it.

HUMBLE BEGINNINGS

I was away in North Carolina at the time when **Married2TheMission** was born, but my heart was set on Birmingham.

I knew that everyone needed help in the world, but my world was where I left it; 2 hours by plane, 15 hours by train, and eight hours south by car.

My world was Birmingham. We tried everything to make it work.

Conference calls, social media, and video-chatting all acted as the glue that held the budding non-profit organization together.

I would put blasts up on social media, and our members would get together to discuss ideas on how to fund social events, community service, and conferences for less fortunate women in Birmingham.

Women called in from all over the place.
Everyone was so excited to be doing something that could benefit the community, and especially women.
I mailed out minutes and ideas. I kept a pink notebook of all my dreams and plans.

Until it dawned on me; I needed to be back home if I was ever going to get serious about what I started. I had to go where my heart was.

I moved back to Birmingham in the spring of 2015.

PASSION FOR THE PAVEMENT

Moving back to Birmingham determined to make M2M a movement for all, I was one focused lady in 2015.

Whether it was library meetings, feeding the homeless, or house meetings M2M was about take off.

You know you have a passion for a cause when you can do it broke.

No matter the cost, I was determined to see **Married2TheMission** thrive.

I took my last earnings and bought t-shirts, supported other non-profit organizations, and made small footprints throughout Birmingham serving wherever I was called.
In light of limited financial support, I would often hold empowerment meetings in my unfurnished apartment.

Meetings would range from various issues of importance: *self esteem, identity, purpose, etc.*

Seeing various women from all walks of life come together inspired me to do more.

With my eyes, I witnessed women getting free from emotional bondage that gripped them for years.

I often thought to myself If this could be accomplished in a living room of a small apartment, what could we do with a building?

I DREAM OF CARRAWAY

It was the mere genius of Dr. Charles N. Carraway to place the city's first major Trauma Hospital in the Norwood community in 1908.

Its presence is monumental. Standing solitude behind gated bars and plush green grass; anyone who looks upon Carraway, even in its present state can't help but to dream.

A medical sanctuary of its day, Carraway hospital was a leading staple in the care of patients with various ailments in the city of Birmingham before it became totally abandoned in the mid 2000's.

Able to nest over 617 patients comfortably,it's real estate stretches several blocks throughout North Birmingham.

Rumoured to be owned by several other non-profit organizations and facilities, Carraway has the potential to be a "major answer" to some of Birmingham's biggest problems.

Naturally, I dreamt daily of how many people I could help there, and still do.

Recreation: the action of recreating something again.

In 2007, I took a visit to a prominent women's rehabilitation facility located in Birmingham, Al.

To date, I believe this center is one of the bigger recreational and rehabilitation centers we have for women here in Birmingham.

 Outside of the YMCA ,The FOUNDRY, etc. It hosts a vast amount of women with various deficiencies.

Catering to victims of diverse circumstance; drug-addiction ,homelessness, etc. The women are housed, fed, resourced, and aided with rehabilitation for an allotted time.

My first visit there was painful. As a woman who had been broken and unstable myself, I wondered how could anyone get free here?

The staff was nice, the people were friendly, the intention was needed, but the environment was not conducive enough to facilitate substantial change.

How is one motivated to change their mind and surroundings if where they are, looks just like where they have been?

Respectfully, the place looked as if it had been run down for years. Everyone was doing the very best they could. Yet no one seemed to be truly free.

I couldn't help but to think that they, and so many more people deserve better.

Recreation and Rehabilitation facilities cannot afford to be a *"laxed project"*.

Tax dollars and other resources fund non profit organizations.
It is a poor representation of what can be done with funds from our city when the places where help is supposed to be received, looks like it needs help itself.

There are about 125 shelters or resource centers throughout Birmingham, and none of them host a state-of-the-art recreational facility.

"In My Father's house there are many mansions. And if not so, would I have told you that I go to prepare a place for you."

John 14:2

CARRAWAY HOSPITAL
MARRIED 2 THE MISSION AND MORE

Malls are effortlessly resourceful in sales because they offer a variance in retail selection by eliminating the inconvenience of having to drive to several different stores.

I believe that the property where Carraway sits has the potential of being the same benefit to several, *if not ALL non-profit organizers and rehabilitation centers throughout the city of Birmingham.*

Blocks away from UAB, one of the most prominent medical hospitals in the nation, **Carraway has the capacity to be revitalized as a state of the art recreational and rehabilitation facility for the homeless, the mentally ill, and the drug addict.**

Married2theMission itself would act as a dormitory style facility that would improve, empower, and facilitate resource for more than 1000 women at a time.

With accessibility to onsite doctors and staff that specialize in mental illness, drug rehabilitation, and abuse counselors.

We would extend care and shelter to pregnant teens who are homeless . Everyone deserves a place to be. Everyone deserves a second chance.

Real healing would have an opportunity to take place, all while creating a REAL possibility of Birmingham residents becoming whole.

Career training, therapy, resume writing, community service projects, etiquette, gymnasiums, technology training, and vocational certifications; would be just a small portion of what would be available to those who need the help in Birmingham via Married2theMission.

Agricultural opportunities could be a major reality to improve the need for local community health. As the landscape at Carraway Hospital permits enough room to start several vegetable gardens.

Due to the influx in the population of latin american citizens here in Birmingham, the facility can also act as a "hub" to learn spanish, and aid in resourcing women who have language barriers, but need the help.

The property, being expansive can serve other non-profit organizations who wish to facilitate recreation for others who also need premier care in other areas. (the elderly, men, etc.)

The positive use of the property would attract as much good attention and money to the city as any other entertainment sector, because of its humanitarian aspect, and uncommon revitalization.

Partnerships with the local hospitals, schools, and the need for security and medical diversified staff would bring several jobs to the city.

Birmingham communities would benefit from the accessibility of resource and care for people who cannot afford basic or advanced aid in revamping their life.

This kind of "community staple center" would keep people off of the street and into their purpose.

Carraway Hospital as a whole would manage to take care of the mandate of Christ, and the answer of the cry here in Birmingham. *With one property the possibilities are endless.*

Imagine how many troubled souls would put a gun down if they knew that there was a better way?

Imagine how many poor people could be innovators if they had the resources?

Imagine how many drug addicted people would be free if quality rehabilitation was accessible?

Imagine how many of those with mental illness could be free if there was a place to heal, and be themselves?

Imagine how many people would believe in GOD or in themselves if Christianity was a helping hand beyond "preaching"?

Imagine how many people would reconsider crime in our city; if we considered their needs first?

Imagine if this wasn't just a dream, but A REALITY?

Can I count on your help?

"On hearing this, Jesus said, "It is not the healthy who need a doctor, but the sick". - Matthew 9:12

I have a dream….. By Shadaria Allison

I have a dream that Birmingham can be.
A star shining a blaze for the world to see.
Buildings, people, freedom, light
A place where wrong surrenders to the courage of what is right.
I have a dream of people taking hands
Of Bold generations willing to take a stand
I have a dream of southern charm redefined
Of Birmingham being glasses for all those that are blind
I have a dream of a better tomorrow
Of civil leaders bringing joy where there was once sorrow
I have a dream of girls being women
A place where the past is the past and all is forgiven.

I have a dream of a wondrous place
Where the privilege is only a smile and never a race
I have a dream of heaven on earth
A place where guidance mirrors the beauty of all self worth
I have a hope of a dream where I find all minds reminiscing
Where women become wed daily
Married2theMission.

About the Author

Shadaria A.Allison is the compelling author of several published manuscripts, motivational speaker, communications strategist, and brand ambassador.

She has been reputed to be a "razor sharp" voice of truth, activist / advocate for women, and charismatic leader of her time. Diversely gifted in the "arts", Shadaria Allison has the components of a star, with a bona-fide sense of humility and wisdom beyond her years.

"Wise as a serpent, Harmless as a Dove": A woman's manual has proven to be a "life changing" body of work as it has afforded Shadaria various speaking opportunities with "ministry elites" such as Church of the Highlands, by way of the C.R.O.W.N organization (a non-profit organization that cater to community needs throughout the inner city of Birmingham.)

There, she was presented with one of many awards for outstanding services; and lasting contributions. (2016)

Shadaria has also featured as a speaker at various events, and workshops throughout Alabama.

Her most recent to date; the *"Equal Pay Movement"* in Fairfield AL. There, she delivered a prolific message on women's rights in an Ever changing economy.

Having almost 10,000 followers on diversified media networking sites, superior reviews on Amazon.com, and several requests for her literary and professional approach; Shadaria's expertise is in high demand.

Her work has been noted to receive great responses on various generational scales, and continues break barriers with raving reviews from all genres alike. Thus, has gained her several requests on projects that require a "fresh" perspective.

Certified in journalism, print media, and mental health studies; Shadaria has proven that writing and the "good of her fellow man" is her passion, and some of the many ways she contributes to both culture and business society.

Shadaria served as main contributor for Femme Plus Magazine (2016). A virtual magazine that offers information and positive trends,outlooks, and encouragement for the plus sized woman.

Shadaria is also staffed in the entertainment industry. A Featured supporting staff in film and various assignments via Central and CAB casting, and has worked with universal pictures.

All by which has granted her to work alongside Hollywood elites such as "Jada Pinkett Smith" and "Queen Latifah".

Owner of ROSE-GOLD cosmetics, LLC. A beauty consulting business geared to steward the female community with counsel, styling, and collective freelance makeup services.

Shadaria has also served as a Plus size model.

She is rapidly becoming a "flourishing" social media personality. Beauty doesn't out scale her wit and compassion for people as:

Shadaria Allison is also seen as a profitable help in her community where she serves as founder of "Married2theMission": an organization whose sole mission is to promote and celebrate the welfare and success of all women by way of empowerment and community service.

A proud member of the "Birmingham Civil Rights Foot Soldiers" in Birmingham Al. Shadaria is a Civil Rights Activist.

An active member of one of many Birmingham community social organizations such as:

"The Sisterhood" ; a non profit organization that feeds a number of local less fortunate residents; and facilitates engagements that inspire women to become more active in community reform.

Shadaria is currently inspiring an "Equal Pay Movement" on behalf of women earning less than satisfiable means of economy, sanctioned under the "Equal Pay Act"(1963) By which she has successfully gathered 100 signatures petitioning the President of the United States to enforce Equal Pay to all women in America via Change.org.

She has served countless hours of community service with bravery, and dedication.

Books By Shadaria Allison

Wise As A Serpent, Harmless As A Dove: A Woman's Manual

(2015)

"The Little Book of Know It Must's": Nuggets Of Wisdom

(2015)

"Poetic Vices: Love. Freedom. Stanzas"

(2016)

"The Whore In Our Worship"

(2017)

Available on Amazon.com

COMING SOON…

DOMESTIC VIOLENCE: THE FEAR OF FEMALE LEADERSHIP IN AMERICA (re-release)

Contact:

Shadaria Allison

Married2TheMission.com

Married2TheMission@gmail.com